W9-BLR-556

Solar Cell and Renewable ENERGY Experiments

Electric Motor Experiments

ISBN 978-0-7660-3306-1

Radio-Controlled Car Experiments

ISBN 978-0-7660-3304-7

Robot Experiments

ISBN 978-0-7660-3303-0

Solar Cell and Renewable Energy Experiments

ISBN 978-0-7660-3305-4

Cool
Science Projects
with
Technology

Solar Cell and Renewable ENERGY Experiments

Ed Sobey, PhD

Enslow Publishers, Inc.
40 Industrial Road
Box 398
Berkeley Heights, NJ 07922
USA

http://www.enslow.com

To Rod and Joyce Brown, two people with continuously renewable energy.

Acknowledgments

Thank you, Rich Sidwa, for the great photograph of the Wind Farm in Montana.
I thank Michael Arquin of KidWind for providing two of the wind turbines shown in this book,
and the valuable information on wind power. Madeline Binder provided a Picoturbine
Windmill kit. I enjoyed assembling it and testing it. Very cool. Thank you, Madeline. The design
for the electric generator came from William Beaty's great web site, Science Hobbyist.
Boonshoft Nature Museum in Dayton, Ohio, built one of the waterwheels shown.

Library of Congress Cataloging-in-Publication Data

Sobey, Edwin J. C., 1948–
    Solar cell and renewal energy experiments / Ed Sobey.
        p. cm. —(Cool science projects with technology)
    Includes bibliographical references and index.
    ISBN 978-0-7660-3305-4
    1. Renewable energy sources—Juvenile literature. 2. Electric power production—Juvenile
    literature. I. Title.
    TJ808.2.S6625 2011
    621.042078—dc22   2010027430

Printed in the United States of America

122010 Lake Book Manufacturing, Inc., Melrose Park, IL

10 9 8 7 6 5 4 3 2 1

To Our Readers: We have done our best to make sure all Internet addresses in this book were
active and appropriate when we went to press. However, the author and the publisher have
no control over and assume no liability for the material available on those Internet sites or
on other Web sites they may link to. Any comments or suggestions can be sent by e-mail to
comments@enslow.com or to the address on the back cover.

♻ Enslow Publishers, Inc., is committed to printing our books on recycled paper. The paper
in every book contains 10% to 30% post-consumer waste (PCW). The cover board on the
outside of each book contains 100% PCW. Our goal is to do our part to help young people and
the environment too!

Photo Credits: All photos by Ed Sobey, except by Deb Green/Big River Resources, LLC , p. 20;
Nick Cobbing/Greenpeace. p. 13; Rich Sidwa, p. 80; The Hagley Museum and Library, p. 104;
U.S. Bureau of Reclamation, p. 106; .

Cover Photos: PunchStock (girl); Ed Sobey (solar cell).

Contents

Experiments with a 🏅 symbol feature Ideas for Your Science Fair.

Experiments with a ✹ symbol feature Ideas for Your Science Fair.

Renewable Energy— An Introduction

Renewable energy is energy that comes from sources that are naturally replenished in short periods of time. Since the sun shines every day, and rain falls and winds blow, these are good choices for energy that will not run out. Energy from tides can also be harnessed. It takes many centuries, however, to replenish the oil, coal, and gas that we use for most of our energy today. Because these nonrenewable energy sources were created a long time ago, they are called fossil fuels.

There is a limited quantity of fossil fuels, though, and a growing need for energy. People are looking to use more renewable sources of energy. In general, renewable energy creates less pollution than fossil fuels. Smoke fumes from burning fossil fuels increase air pollution and probably contribute to global warming.

During your lifetime, you could see great changes in how energy is provided and used. You could even contribute your ideas through the research you conduct. This book will get you started.

Science Fair Projects

Solar and other renewable energy projects can make great science fair entries. With the world turning more attention to energy issues, your project could be quite popular.

Throughout this book, there are suggested experiments to try. Any of them could become a science fair project. Better yet, you could take one of these ideas and change it to make your own project.

To create a great science fair project, you need to understand the rules. Each contest has different criteria, and each has its own forms and rules. Make sure that you know the rules before investing time and energy in your project.

A great way to think about a science fair project on renewable energy is to think of something fun that will end up giving you two things, or variables, you can measure and compare. Light power (wattage of lightbulbs) used to power a photovoltaic cell could be compared to the output electric power, for example. When you can measure two variables, where one influences the other, you get a set of data you can graph. Graphs visually tell the story of your project and show the relationship between the two variables. Judges like to see that you collected measurable data, analyzed them, and graphed them.

Of course, you have to follow good science practices.

Your integrity as a scientist is most important. Report what you did and what happened, not what you wanted to happen. Make one change to your experiment at a time and measure its impact before making another change.

Keep good notes. If you are not a natural note taker, work especially hard at recording everything. Where possible, take photographs of your experiments in progress. Record where you got information and materials. Write down your ideas when you think of them—before they vanish.

The most important point is to pick a project that is fun for you. If it's fun, you will spend more time working on it, and you will do a better job. Researchers play for a living. They pick what sounds interesting to them and they figure out ways to learn something new about it. You should do the same. Start with your interests and build on them.

The Scientific Method

You can run many great experiments with renewable energy, but to use these in a scientific report or science fair, you need to follow a few guidelines. Conducting a scientific experiment includes making observations, measuring variables, collecting and analyzing data, researching literature, and producing an attractive and easy-to-understand report. Simply making a model isn't science.

Start your project by learning to use circuits and solar cells. This is the best way to learn. Ask yourself how they operate and what they can do. As you learn more, ask yourself more detailed questions. Before running the experiment, think of a possible answer or hypothesis. The experiment can test whether your hypothesis is correct.

A good question is one that you can answer by running a test and collecting data (information, often in measurements). Being able to represent that data in a graph helps people understand what you have discovered. As you conduct experiments, remember to change only one variable at a time. If you change more than one variable at once, you won't be able to tell which one caused the effects you see.

Experiment Notebook

Keep a notebook in which you record information about each experiment you conduct. Each entry you add should have a date so that you can keep track of when you did each experiment. List the materials you use, and keep notes on what you try and what results you observe. Add sketches of designs and circuits that you use. Add photos if you can. This is what scientists, engineers, and inventors do, and so should you. You will be able to build on these notes for a long, long time.

Safety First

1. Do any experiments or projects, whether from this book or of your own design, under the supervision of a science teacher or other knowledgeable adult.

2. Read all instructions carefully before proceeding with a project. If you have questions, check with your supervisor before going any further.

3. Maintain a serious attitude while conducting experiments. Fooling around can be dangerous to you and to others.

4. Wear approved safety goggles when you are working with a flame or chemicals or doing anything that might cause injury to your eyes.

5. Have a first aid kit nearby while you are experimenting.

6. Do not put your fingers or any object other than properly designed electrical connectors into electrical outlets.

7. Never let water droplets come in contact with a hot lightbulb.

8. Do not eat or drink while experimenting.

9. Always wear shoes, not sandals, while experimenting.

10. The liquid in some thermometers is mercury (a dense liquid metal). It is dangerous to touch mercury or breathe

mercury vapor, and such thermometers have been banned in many states. When doing these experiments, use only non-mercury thermometers, such as those filled with alcohol. If you have a mercury thermometer in the house, ask an adult if it can be taken to a local thermometer exchange location.

Where Does Energy Come From?

You use energy every day. Energy fuels your body, and the car, bus, or train you ride. It heats and cools your home and school, and powers all the appliances you use. Where does this energy come from?

Sunlight is the ultimate source of nearly all the energy on planet Earth. In addition to heat, the sun provides energy for plants to grow. Then these plants provide energy for animals. When the plants and animals die, they can become the fossil energy found in coal, gas, and oil. The sun's heat also causes winds to blow. Winds drive ocean currents and waves. Almost everything that moves, makes sound, or lights up relies on solar energy as its ultimate source.

FIGURE 1 Iceland leads the world in generating electricity from geothermal sources. Over 25 percent of Iceland's electricity and over 85 percent of its heating needs come from geothermal energy. This plant in Iceland extracts heat from the earth for heating and other uses.

Most of the energy that is not supplied by the sun comes from the breakdown of radioactive material and from geothermal (heat from the earth) sources (Figure 1).

Radioactive materials probably originated from outside our solar system in the explosions of giant stars called supernovas. Geothermal energy comes from decay of radioactive materials and from the heat generated during the formation of the planet. Neither of these sources provides as much energy as the sun.

What Powers Your Life?

What are the primary energy types that you use? Electricity and transportation fuel (probably gasoline) are the predominant ones. In the United States, nearly half of the electricity is generated by burning coal. Where does the electricity you use every day come from?

1. Ask your family about the utility company that provides your electricity. See if the utility Web site shows how and where they generate electricity. If they don't produce electricity themselves, they purchase it from one or several other companies. See if you can track down how these companies make electricity.

2. Ask to see your family's electric bill. Does it show you which suppliers your family uses?

    Where does the electrical energy you use come from? Does it come from renewable or nonrenewable sources?

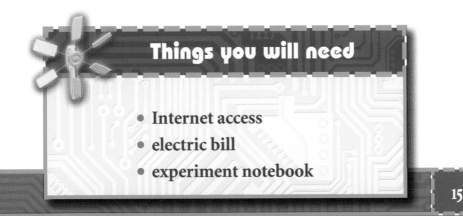

Things you will need

- Internet access
- electric bill
- experiment notebook

Nonrenewable Energy in the United States

More than 90 percent of energy in the United States comes from nonrenewable sources. Coal is the largest source of this power. It is created over long periods of time, hundreds of millions of years, as dead plant matter is compressed within the earth. A one-foot-thick layer of coals requires up to seven feet of compacted plant matter. With heat and pressure, the plant matter, largely made of carbon, is transformed first into peat and later into coal. This series of physical and chemical reactions is called coalification.

Burning coal today releases solar energy that plants had captured about 300 million years ago. So coal is a form of stored solar energy. It will renew as plants today die and are buried, but this won't occur on human time scales. It will take another 300 million years to replace the coal we are burning today. For this reason, coal is classified as a solar, nonrenewable energy source.

The second largest source of power for electric energy in the United States comes from nuclear generators (about 20 percent). In this case the fuel is radioactive material—enriched uranium. Uranium does not come from the sun. It was created along with some other elements in the explosions of supernovas billions of years ago.

In providing energy for electricity, natural gas is close

behind nuclear generation. Like coal, natural gas is a fossil fuel—a fuel formed long ago by the anaerobic (without oxygen) decay of plant material. Oil and gas are formed by the same process as coal. They form underground in areas called "fields" from which they are pumped to the surface and used. Although there are undoubtedly many places on earth where oil, gas, and coal are forming today, our use of these fuels far exceeds the rate of replenishment. All three are termed nonrenewable.

Renewable Energy in the United States

Generating electricity at dams (hydroelectric generation) accounts for about 9 percent of the total electricity generation in the United States. Where does the energy come from? What lifts the water into the mountains so that it can fall to lower elevations and generate electricity? This too is a result of the sun. The earth is a giant heat engine fueled by solar radiation. This engine evaporates water from the seas, lakes, rivers, and land, and redistributes it across the globe. Some of the falling rain and snow lands on mountains. This water has an increased potential energy because it has been raised above sea level. Like lifting a Slinky spring toy to the top of the stairs, the increased elevation gives it energy to slink down the stairs. When water is captured in reservoirs behind dams, we can release it in a controlled manner through electrical generators that convert this water pressure into electrical energy. This is solar energy that renews itself with every rainstorm and snowstorm.

Energy Around the World

Most countries burn oil and gas to make electrical energy. However, each country and region inside a country may use them in different percentages. Some countries get all their electrical energy by burning fossil fuels (Trinidad and Tobago, for example). France gets a very large percentage (75 percent) of its electricity from nuclear reactors. Norway, blessed with tall mountains and a wet climate, gets essentially all of its electricity from water power captured at dams. Each country uses the most affordable energy sources available to it.

Future Renewable Energy

There are several other renewable energy sources that so far have not played a large role in meeting our energy needs. These include geothermal, wind, tides and waves, ocean thermal, and biofuels.

Geothermal energy is derived from heat that is produced inside Earth. This heat is a byproduct of radioactive decay of naturally occurring materials such as uranium. Although this energy is free to use, it is difficult to capture. As a source of energy, it is much weaker than the sun.

Wind energy production is growing rapidly throughout the world and especially in the United States. Wind is a form of solar energy. The sun's radiation heats the earth. As air warms, it rises. The air moves in patterns that control climate and weather. Wind turbines can now capture wind energy and convert it into electricity nearly as cheaply as energy is made by burning coal.

Additional sources of renewable energy are found at sea. The rhythmic rise and fall of tides can be used in some locations to provide energy to generate electricity. Tides occur when the gravity of the moon and sun pull on water. As the earth turns, this attraction causes water to move. The shape of some bays funnels water into large flows that can be used to generate electricity.

Waves, increasingly, are viewed as a source of energy. They are another form of solar power since they are generated by wind, which is caused by solar heating. Therefore, wind and wave energy are renewable, solar energy sources. Although waves around the world have tremendous power, capturing the power of the sea has proved difficult.

The ocean and especially polar seas offer the prospect of generating electricity by using large temperature differences.

In the Tropics, ocean surface temperatures can be 30 degrees C (86 degrees F), while only a few thousand meters below the surface the water temperature is nearly freezing. In polar seas, air temperatures above the sea ice can be –40 degrees C (–40 degrees F), while the temperature of the water immediately beneath the ice is at or slightly below freezing. These temperature differences are large enough to power heat engines, but this has not yet proven to be a reliable source of energy.

The last category of energy is biofuels (Figure 2). This is, in essence, capturing the sun's energy in plants and converting this stored energy to a usable fuel. This is like making coal without the 300-million-year wait. The heat and gas generated in a compost pile are two examples of biofuel energy. In the United States, there is currently a rush to grow crops (principally corn) that can be converted into substitutes for gasoline. In 2010, it took almost a gallon of petroleum to power the farmer's tractor and fertilize the crop

FIGURE 2

An ethanol plant in West Burlington, Iowa, ferments the sugars found in crops to make ethyl alcohol. Ethyl alcohol can replace gasoline in vehicles.

to grow corn that produces a gallon of alternate fuel. Making this process more energy efficient will speed the adoption of biofuels.

The high cost of using alternative energy has kept people from using them. But as fossil fuels (coal, gas, and oil) become scarcer and demand for energy continues to rise, more effort is being made to find substitutes. In addition to declining energy sources, environmental concerns about climate-changing emissions from burning fossil fuels are driving us to explore renewable energy sources. Scientists believe that humans have negatively impacted the climate and that life-changing consequences await us if we fail to lower the emissions from burning fossil fuels.

Although predictions about the future are impossible to make with accuracy, we can predict with some certainty that during your lifetime you will see major changes in energy sources and how they are used.

There is more than enough renewable energy available to power all of our needs for a long time to come. The challenges are how to capture and convert that energy into something we can use. As a research scientist or engineer, you can play a role in helping to solve these technological problems. Let's do some research!

Using Electricity

ook around you to find all the places that electric energy can be found. Every room of every building is loaded with electrical outlets, fixtures, and switches. We are in the electric age.

It wasn't always this way. Before 1881, electricity was a laboratory curiosity. In that year, the first public electric service was launched in England. Thomas Edison started his first steam-powered electric generator to provide public power in the United States in 1882. Even after these industry firsts, it was not certain that electricity would become the most important power source. People had been using gas lamps and factories had been powered by stream mills and steam. In factories, power was sent from one place to another by leather belts or by long metal shafts and gears. Many people did not see any reason to change to using electricity.

However, electricity met people's needs so well, it displaced the other energy sources. It is amazingly versatile, able to power computers and television sets, cook food, and heat homes. It is easy to transport over tens of miles or even hundreds of miles. Power generators can be built near the fuel sources (at dams for hydroelectric power, near sources of cooling water for nuclear power, and near mines for coal-fired plants), which saves money. The only difficulty with electric power is storing it. Making huge storage batteries would be too expensive, so electricity has to be used as it is being generated.

Another benefit of electricity is that as technology changes and new—and hopefully renewable—sources become available, they can feed into the existing distribution system that carries electricity. Converting solar, geothermal, tidal, or wind energy into electricity to replace power plants that burn fossil fuels is the main focus of current efforts.

Before we do experiments with renewable energy, let's get familiar with electricity and electric circuits. The skills and experience you gain in these experiments will help you conduct experiments in later chapters.

Make an Electric Circuit

All the materials for this experiment are available at electronic stores and in science catalogs. The motor and clip leads will cost less than the battery, so total expenditures will be a few dollars.

1. To get a DC toy motor to work, touch the two terminals on the motor to the two battery terminals of a 9-volt battery. The motor terminals are small silver tabs on one end. You will hear, feel, and possibly see the motor shaft spinning. Try it the other way: Flip the motor around so that its terminals are touching the opposite terminals on the battery. What do you notice?

Either way you connect the motor to the battery, the motor works. But, you might notice that the motor shaft turns in the opposite direction when you reverse the connection to the battery.

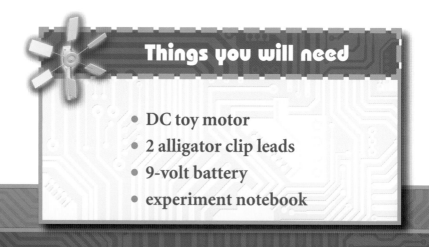

Things you will need

- **DC toy motor**
- **2 alligator clip leads**
- **9-volt battery**
- **experiment notebook**

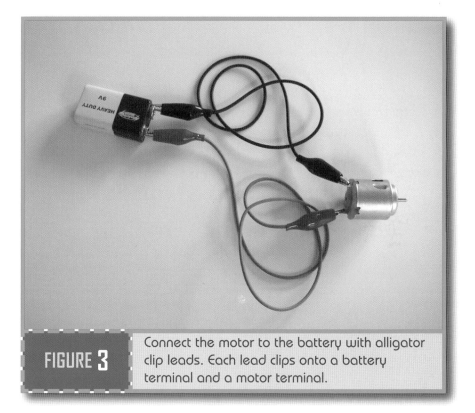

FIGURE 3

FIGURE 3 Connect the motor to the battery with alligator clip leads. Each lead clips onto a battery terminal and a motor terminal.

2. Now use the clip leads to connect the motor to the battery (Figure 3). The motor should work as it did before. Sometimes you will find a defective clip lead, in which case no electricity will flow. If that occurs, replace one clip lead with another and figure out which one is bad.

If you got the motor to spin, you made a complete circuit (Figure 4). Electricity won't flow unless the circuit is complete, or closed. The electric charges flowing through the wires need a return path to the battery.

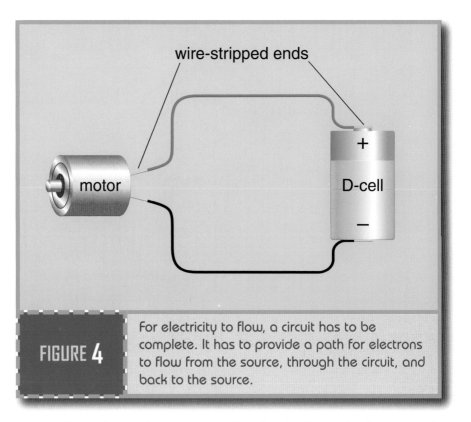

wire-stripped ends

motor

+

D-cell

−

FIGURE 4

For electricity to flow, a circuit has to be complete. It has to provide a path for electrons to flow from the source, through the circuit, and back to the source.

Complete circuits are the basis for all the electric appliances you use. Most don't use batteries, which supply direct current (DC). Instead, they use alternating current (AC). AC is delivered through wires directly to the appliance, as in overhead lights, or through electric outlets mounted in building walls.

Many of the activities in this book will center on replacing the battery with a renewable source of electricity. But before we get to those, let's make some measurements.

Measure the Voltage of a Battery

COOL!

A 9-volt battery delivers approximately, but not exactly, 9 volts of electricity if it is fresh. With use, it will deliver a lower voltage. Let's measure the voltage.

You can purchase a voltmeter or multimeter (Figure 5) at an electronics store or from a science catalog for a few dollars. Or you might be able to borrow one from your school.

1. Turn the dial on the meter so that DC Volts (or DCV) is underneath the arrow. If the meter offers several scales or voltage ranges, pick one that includes at least 20 volts.

2. Touch the ends of the meter's two probes (wires with metal tips—one is black and the other is red) to the two battery terminals and read the meter. Record the reading in an experiment notebook.

Did you get a negative number? Try switching the probes to the other battery terminals. Electrons flow from the negative terminal of the battery through a complete circuit and

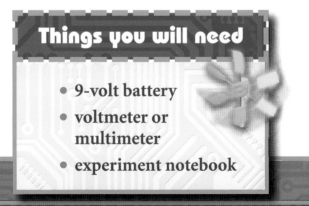

Things you will need

- **9-volt battery**
- **voltmeter or multimeter**
- **experiment notebook**

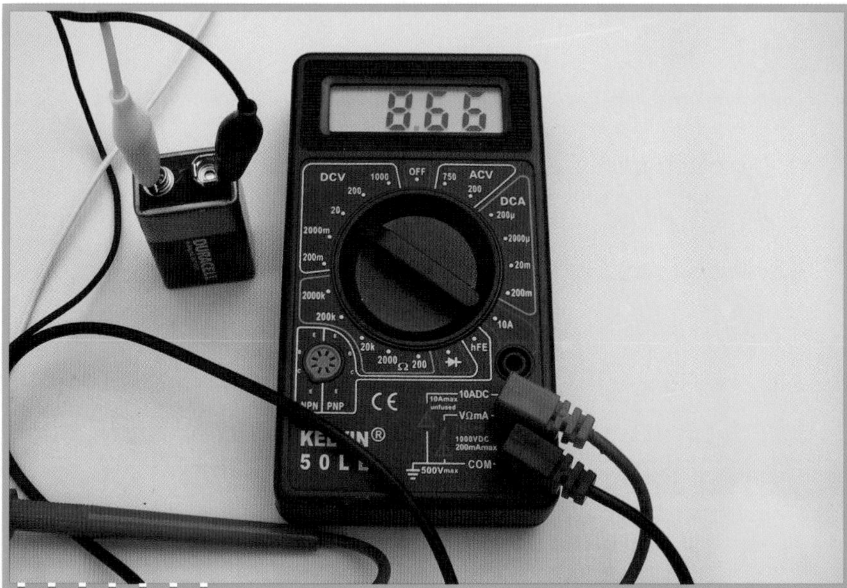

FIGURE 5   Use a voltmeter or multimeter to measure the voltage and current in circuits.

back to the positive terminal. If only one of the probes touches the battery, electricity cannot flow. We say that the circuit is open. Closing the circuit by connecting both probes allows electrons to move.

When the red lead is connected to the positive side of a circuit or battery and the black lead to the negative side, the meter will give a positive value. The meter will work with the leads in the reverse position, but the value will be negative.

Check out the side of the battery to see which terminal is marked with a "+" and which is marked "–".

Measure the Voltage in a Circuit

Voltage is how much force the battery can exert to push electrons through a circuit. The battery you are using has a potential electric force of 9 volts. But until you put it into a complete circuit, the force isn't doing anything and the electrons are not flowing. To get a better feel for the potential electric force, let's put the battery to work.

1. Connect the electric motor to a 9-volt battery with two alligator clip leads.

2. Now measure the voltage across the battery terminals. With the voltmeter dial turned to the 20-volt setting, touch the red lead to the positive terminal of the battery. Touch the black lead to the negative terminal. Record this value. Is it different from the measurement you made in the previous experiment when the battery was not in a circuit?

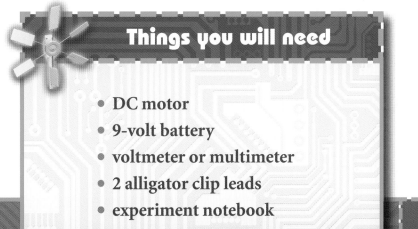

Things you will need

- DC motor
- 9-volt battery
- voltmeter or multimeter
- 2 alligator clip leads
- experiment notebook

Idea for a Science Fair Project

Using a voltmeter, you can measure the drop in a battery's voltage as it powers a DC motor. Keeping the circuit open, measure the voltage every minute for at least ten minutes and graph the result. Compare this voltage timeline to that of the same battery made by a different company or to a different type of battery (carbon, alkaline, lithium, NiCDs, or other). Add timelines to the graph for each battery you test. Which provides the steadiest voltage? You could also add the price per battery to your analysis to decide which battery offers the best value.

When a battery supplies electric power to a motor or light, the voltage you recorded will be a more accurate measure of its potential force. As batteries get used, they lose the ability to produce electricity. The voltage they produce is reduced. However, you don't see that when measuring voltages that aren't loaded (connected in a circuit).

Measure Current

Voltage describes potential electric force in a circuit. *Amperes*, or *amps*, measure the current, or flow of electricity. An ammeter counts the number of charges (units of electricity) that go through the unit each second. Multimeters measure volts and amps. Some voltmeters will measure amps as well as volts.

To remember the difference between volts and amps, picture a water tower with a hose coming out the bottom. The taller the tower is and the deeper the water is inside, the more water pressure is available. Water pressure is analogous to electric voltage.

The pressure (or voltage) can be quite high, but until you open the valve (or complete the circuit), there is no flow of water (or electricity). If the valve is only slightly open, the

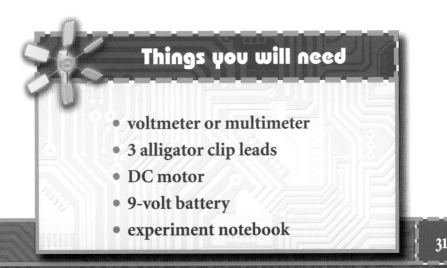

Things you will need

- voltmeter or multimeter
- 3 alligator clip leads
- DC motor
- 9-volt battery
- experiment notebook

flow (or current) will be low, even if the potential (or voltage) is quite high. Constrictions in the hose (or resistance in the circuit) can also reduce the current. On the other hand, even if the potential is low, a huge hose (or good conductor) will allow a large amount of water (or current) to pass.

Let's measure the electric current in a circuit.

1. Check to see if your voltmeter measures electric current—some do not. On the dial, look for marking *DCA*, which stands or "Direct Current Amperes." If your meter has this, look at the ranges available to use. Choose a current range that goes up to 10A.

   You might have to move the leads to different plugs on the meter to allow you to measure current. Check the printed instructions that came with the meter or look at the face of the meter for diagrams that indicate the position of the plugs.

2. Remove one alligator clip lead from the battery. Connect this to one of the meter probes. Use the third clip lead to complete the circuit by connecting the second meter probe to the open battery terminal. This should result in a series circuit or loop that connects the battery to the motor, the motor to the voltmeter, and the voltmeter to the other battery terminal (Figure 6).

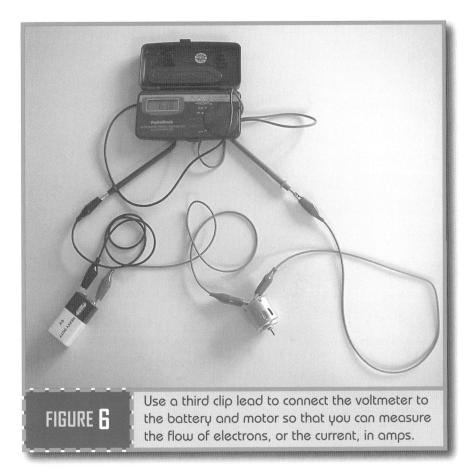

FIGURE 6

Use a third clip lead to connect the voltmeter to the battery and motor so that you can measure the flow of electrons, or the current, in amps.

3. Switch the meter to the position that measures current and complete the circuit so that the motor spins.

4. Read the meter. How much current does the meter show? Record this value in your experiment notebook, along with a description of the experiment you are running. Make sure you label the numeric value with the units, amps.

Motors draw a lot of current. This battery will be expended in a short time if you leave it connected to the motor, so disconnect it when you are finished making your observations.

Idea for a Science Fair Project

With a handful of resistors with different values (from an electronics store) you could measure the current in a simple circuit with different resistors. Graph the current against the value of the resistor used in the circuit for a 9-volt battery. To be sure that the battery doesn't lose significant power while you are running the experiment, repeat the first test for the first resistor after testing all the others to see if the current is the same. Then test the resistance of other nonliving objects you can find. Place them in the circuit, measure the current, and enter the value on your graph. You might test an aluminum pie pan, a fork, or a nail.

How Much Power Is Your Motor Using?

Many appliances you use list their electric usage in watts. Watts are the units of measurement for power. You know that a 100-watt bulb is brighter than a 60-watt bulb. The 100-watt bulb uses more power and converts that electric power into heat and light, both of which are types of energy.

When the bill for your household electricity comes, check it out. You are charged for the amount of electricity you use. This is measured in kilowatt-hours. A kilowatt is 1,000 watts. A kilowatt-hour is the amount of energy in one kilowatt of power used for one hour. Let's calculate the power your motor is using.

In an electric circuit, power can be calculated as:

$$\textbf{Power} = \textbf{Voltage} \times \textbf{Current}$$

or, stated in the units we measure:

$$\textbf{Watts} = \textbf{volts} \times \textbf{amps}$$

Things you will need

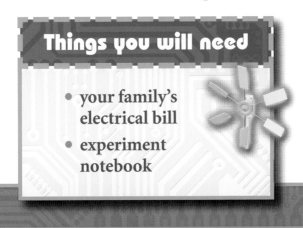

- your family's electrical bill
- experiment notebook

Insert into this equation the measurements you made of voltage under load (while the motor was running) and the current (measured in amps). Calculate and record in your experiment notebook the power (in watts) that your motor is using. The value is probably in the range of 3 to 5 watts.

Generate Electricity

When you generate electricity, you will want to measure the voltage and current you generate so that you can figure out how much power in watts you are making.

Power plants generate electricity by converting mechanical energy into electric energy. The mechanical energy is provided by a spinning turbine. The turbine can be made to spin by rushing water (in the case of a hydroelectric dam) wind, or steam. Nuclear and fossil fuel electric plants produce steam to make mechanical energy. Once the turbine blades are spinning, their motion turns or spins a generator.

The generator is a motor run in reverse. A motor takes electric energy and transforms it into mechanical energy, or motion. A generator takes mechanical energy and transforms it into electric energy. The motor you used in the previous experiments can become a generator.

Things you will need

- DC motor
- alligator clip leads
- experiment notebook
- voltmeter or multimeter

If you spin the motor shaft, you will generate electricity. Not much electricity, however. You need to spin the motor shaft very quickly to generate enough electricity to measure.

1. Wire the motor terminals directly to the voltmeter. Use one alligator clip lead to connect one meter probe to one of the motor terminals and use a second clip lead to connect the other probe to the other motor terminal.

2. Rotate the meter dial to the smallest voltage value scale (DCV).

3. Spin the motor shaft between your fingers. Does the meter register any voltage?

It may help to have a propeller or gear on the motor shaft that you can push. See if you can briefly generate some electricity. Record the largest voltage you are able to generate.

Generate Electricity With a Motor-Generator

To turn the shaft of a motor fast enough to generate a significant voltage, you can connect it to a motor. The combination is called a motor-generator.

You can use a small electric motor to turn the shaft of another motor (Figure 7), which acts as a generator. The challenge is to connect the shafts of the two motors so that the energy of the motor is effectively carried to the generator. There are several ways to do this.

1. Cut a short piece from a small-diameter straw, such as a cocktail straw. Wrap 2 turns of clear tape around the ends of the shafts of two motors. Slide the piece of cocktail

Things you will need

- **2 DC motors**
- **cocktail straw**
- **scissors**
- **duct tape**
- **4 alligator clip leads**
- **1-in by 2-in lumber, 30 cm (12 in) long**
- **clear tape**
- **LED (light-emitting diode)**

FIGURE 7

In a motor-generator, a battery provides power to turn the first motor, and it spins the second motor, which generates electricity.

straw onto the taped shafts. The straw should be a tight fit. If not, add another short piece of tape around the shafts under the straw.

2. Hold both motors to something solid, such as a desk top or piece of wood. In Figure 7, duct tape holds both motors to a piece of 1-in by 2-in lumber. While taping them down, make sure that the motor shafts are in line with each other.

3. Pick one motor to be the generator. Connect this motor to an LED (light-emitting diode). (See Figure 8.) Electronics stores and science catalogs sell LEDs, or you can find them in appliances that you take apart. Use two alligator clip leads to connect the LED to the generator output wires. An LED is a diode, an electronics component that passes electricity in one direction only. If you connect it backward, the LED won't light. It is easy to reconnect

in the correct direction if it does not light up. (See step 5.)

4. Use two more clip leads to connect the second motor to a 9-volt battery. Make sure that the motor is spinning and that the generator is, too. If the connector between the motor and generator is loose, the motor shaft could spin without turning the generator shaft. Of course, if the LED lights up, you know that the generator is working.

FIGURE 8

The generator is creating enough power to light the LED. One motor is powered by the battery, and it turns the shaft of the second motor-generator.

5. If the LED doesn't come on, reverse its leads. That is, take one alligator clip lead off the longer leg of the LED (Did you notice that the two legs or contacts have different lengths?) and put it on the shorter leg. Take the clip lead that was on the shorter leg and put it on the longer leg. If the generator is working, the LED should come on.

The longer leg of an LED goes toward the positive side of the power source and the shorter leg goes to the negative side. You can test this and the LED by touching the legs to the terminals of a 9-volt battery. Briefly touch the long leg to the terminal marked "+" and the short leg to the terminal marked "−." Since the LED isn't made for this much voltage, do not leave it on the battery terminals or it will quickly burn out.

You have just generated electricity and used it to produce light. You've made an electric system. Now let's see how much voltage that system generates.

Use the same setup you used in the Experiment 3.7. In this experiment, you will replace the LED with a voltmeter so that you can measure the output voltage.

1. Use alligator clip leads to connect the motor-generator to the voltmeter probes.

2. Turn the dial on the voltmeter to measure up to 20 volts DC. Turn on the motor and read and record the voltage.

3. Once you have recorded the voltage, reconnect the voltmeter to measure the input voltage of the battery while the motor is running. Record this voltage.

4. Compare the battery voltage you measured to the output voltage of the generator. Did you expect that the two would be the same? Why is the output lower than the input?

Things you will need

- voltmeter or multimeter
- 4 alligator clip leads
- Motor-generator from Experiment 3.7
- experiment notebook

5. Feel the motor and the generator. Even if they have been running for only a short time, you will feel that they are warmer than the air. You heard them spin. Generating the heat and sound took energy and reduced the amount of electric energy that the generator could make.

All machines operate at less than 100 percent efficiency. They experience a loss of energy due to friction, vibrations, or other causes. The higher the efficiency of a machine or system, the less energy it wastes.

To calculate the voltage efficiency of your motor-generator, divide the output voltage by the input voltage. Use the battery voltage you measured, not the rated voltage printed on the side of the battery.

Voltage efficiency = output voltage/input voltage

In a trial of this experiment, we found that the battery was providing 8.7 volts, and the output voltage from the generator was 7.2 volts. Dividing 7.2 volts by 8.7 volts gives a voltage efficiency of 83 percent. For every volt input, the system output 0.83 volts.

Make an Electrical Generator

Inside a motor, an electrical current passes through electromagnets. As the motor spins, the electromagnets switch from positive to negative so they are alternately attracted to and repelled from permanent magnets, which are also located inside the motor. This keeps the motor spinning.

As a generator, the motor works in reverse. Now the mechanical spinning of the motor shaft turns the electromagnets around, under the magnetic fields of the two permanent magnets. Electric current forms in the windings, and as the

Things you will need

- an adult
- cardboard
- scissors
- ruler
- marker or pen
- 4 ceramic magnets (e.g., Radio Shack #64-1887)
- knife (optional)
- large nail
- hot glue
- 30-gauge magnet wire (e.g., Radio Shack # 278-1345)
- sandpaper or steel wool
- piece of wood or plastic to make into a small box
- 2 alligator clip leads
- voltmeter or multimeter
- miniature lamp (Radio Shack #272-1139)
- experiment notebook

windings spin inside, they force them to pump electrons out to the terminals.

The most challenging part in making this generator (see Figure 9) is making the box to hold the spinning magnets. The box needs to be just large enough to allow the magnets to spin. Making the box larger reduces the electricity you generate as the distance between magnets and windings will be larger. If the box too small, it will be impossible to spin the magnets.

1. Cut a strip of cardboard about 8 to 10 cm (3 to 4 in) high and 18 to 20 cm (7 to 8 in) long. Having this cardboard frame too tall is not a problem.

2. Mark a vertical line about $1/2$ cm (1 in) from one of the ends. This line will later be a folded line that you can score with a knife.

3. Lay 4 ceramic magnets out on the cardboard, starting with the line you just drew, so that you can determine how long one side of the box should be. Lay a magnet flat on the cardboard and rotate the magnet around its center. Move the magnet closer to or farther away from the line you drew to give the magnet enough clearance to rotate.

FIGURE 9 This generator was made out of a wooden tea box. The crank spins the magnets inside, and that generates electricity in the wire windings.

4. Mark another vertical line at the other end of the first magnet where you will later fold the cardboard.

5. Stack the four magnets together so that you can estimate how wide the box should be. Leave some extra room, as the magnets will slide around on the nail that will be the axle. Also, the axle will take up some additional room, but not much. When you have estimated the width of the end of the box, mark it with a vertical line.

6. Now mark the other side of the box. For this side, you can just measure the length of the first side and use that measurement for the second side. Make a vertical line to indicate the junction between the second side and the last end piece. Mark the second end piece to be the same length of the first one.

7. Cut away any excess cardboard. **Have an adult** use a knife or one blade of a pair of scissors to score the vertical lines you drew.

8. Mark the center of the two long sides of the box.

9. Use a nail to punch a hole through these two center marks. The nail axle will slide into these holes.

10. Glue the end flaps together to make the box. Let the glue dry.

11. Test it to make sure that the magnets can rotate around the nail. Slide the nail through the holes and put two magnets on one side of the nail. Add the other two on the other side. Push them around so that the nail is in the center of the set of magnets. Is there enough room for them to rotate? If not, make a new slightly larger box. This one will be easier to make since you can measure the sides of the first box and increase the dimensions a bit.

12. Wrap the magnet wire around the box, centered on the

two holes. Tape one end of the wire to the upper side of the box, giving yourself enough room to sand the end of the wire later. Then start winding the wire around the box. As you wind, keep track of the number of windings you make. You should get 200 or more.

13. When, finally, you get to the other end, tape it near the first end.

14. Use some sandpaper or steel wool to strip the enamel insulation off the ends of both wires. You will see the color change when the enamel has been removed.

15. Push aside the windings just enough to get the nail through the holes.

16. If you have a piece of wood or plastic available, make a handle so that it will be easier to turn the magnets.

17. Put the magnets back on the nail and balance them.

18. Using alligator clips, connect the two generator wires to a multimeter. With clip leads, connect the meter probes to the generator wires. Switch the meter to measure DC volts. Slowly turn the nail. You should see voltages registering on the meter. If not, check to see that you got the insulation off the ends of the wires and that they are connected to the meter.

19. Notice that as you turn the magnets, the output voltage

changes sign with each rotation. This is an alternating current, or AC, generator. Each time the magnets spin, they push electrons in one direction and then the other.

20. Switch the meter to measure AC volts on the lowest scale. Spin the magnets as fast as you can to see if you can measure an AC voltage. The meter may not measure AC voltages this low.

21. Connect the miniature light to the generator terminals and see if you can power it. Turn out the room lights and look for a faint glow. The generator won't power your video game, but it can light up a small light.

Consider that it took a lot of work on your part to make even this little bit of electricity. Then look around your house and outside to see how much electricity people use. The generators that power our homes, schools, and factories are huge.

There are other ways to generate electricity, but most of what we use is generated by turning the shafts of large motors. For renewable energy to be most helpful, it needs to provide electricity to the existing system of wires and transformers that power the country.

Solar Power

Nearly all renewable energy comes from the sun. This chapter looks at directly capturing the sun's energy and using it to make electricity. Later chapters cover other systems (wind, hydrological cycle, etc.) that capture the sun's energy before people can tap into it. Systems that convert light energy into electricity are called photovoltaic systems.

Photovoltaics

When photons (particles of light) strike some materials, they free electrons, which can move and create electric current. In most materials, this photovoltaic effect generates very few electrons. But in some materials the effect is significant. Nineteenth-century scientists discovered this effect with several materials, including selenium, a chemical element. In the mid-twentieth century, scientists switched to silicon and achieved much higher rates of energy conversion. This launched the use of photovoltaics as energy sources in the military and space programs.

A photon can pass through a solar cell, reflect off the solar cell, or be absorbed. If absorbed, it can free an electron to move, which creates an electric current.

Silicon solar cells generate up to 0.5 volt. Making a cell larger does not increase its voltage. And, although a cloud passing overhead doesn't significantly reduce the output voltage of a solar cell, the current produced is strongly affected by the level of light hitting the cell.

A voltage of 0.5 is too low to be useful, so a number of solar cells are commonly wired together. Connecting them in a series (the positive terminal of one cell is connected to the negative terminal of the next cell) adds the voltage output of each cell.

We can instead connect them in parallel (each positive terminal is connected to the others, and each negative terminal is connected to the others). The total voltage output will be the same as the voltage of one cell (0.5 volt), but the output current will be much higher.

Silicon solar cells are able to convert about 17 percent of the sunlight they receive into electricity. The highest theoretical percentage is 28 percent. To improve the cells so that they convert a higher percentage of energy will take a lot of research.

To do experiments with solar cells, you will need several cells, alligator clip leads, a light source, multimeter, LEDs, and motors. It would be helpful to have a few different models of solar cells so that you can compare them. Check science catalogs to see what is available.

Measure the Output of a Photovoltaic Cell

1. You can use alligator clip leads to connect one photovoltaic cell to the probes of a multimeter (Figure 10). Although there is no harm in hooking the meter up backward (so that it measures negative volts), find the positive side of the cell (marked with a + or having a red wire lead) and connect that to the positive red probe of the meter. Connect a second clip lead to the negative side of the meter and cell. Switch the meter to measure DC volts in the range of 20v. Record the value you measure.

2. Turn on the lamp. Record the voltage output by the photovoltaic cell. Also record the wattage of the bulb you are

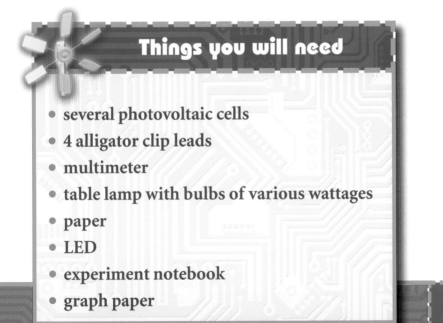

Things you will need

- several photovoltaic cells
- 4 alligator clip leads
- multimeter
- table lamp with bulbs of various wattages
- paper
- LED
- experiment notebook
- graph paper

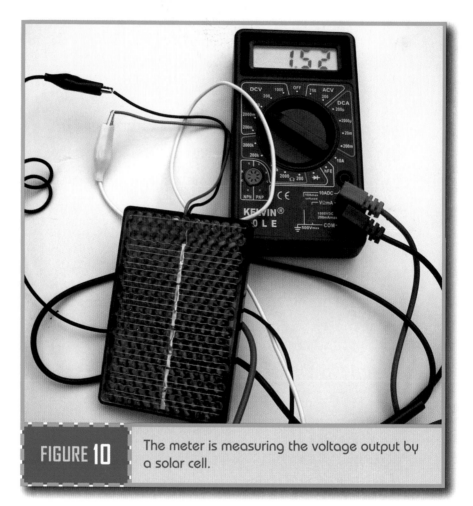

FIGURE 10   The meter is measuring the voltage output by a solar cell.

using. Move the lamp closer to and farther away from the cell. What effect does this have on the output voltage? Block some of the light from the lamp with a piece of paper. Can you see a correlation to the amount of light you block and the output voltage? Describe this experience in your experiment notebook.

3. Collect as many of the different wattage bulbs as you can find that fit the lamp socket. Keeping the position of the lamp and the solar cell the same, try each bulb. Keep the light on only as long as you need to measure the voltage. This will prevent the bulbs from heating up, which would make changing the bulbs difficult. Record your data in your notebook, then graph the data (Figure 11).

4. On your graph, lightly draw a straight line that best fits the data. Calculate the slope of the line by picking two points near each end of the line. The slope of the line is the difference in the output voltage between the two points divided by the difference in the input voltage:

$$\text{Slope} = \frac{(\text{output voltage 2} - \text{output voltage 1})}{(\text{input voltage 2} - \text{input voltage 1})}$$

Look at the graph in Figure 11. We recorded these data using a gooseneck lamp and a variety of incandescent light-bulbs. Note that the very high voltage recorded for the 50 watts was generated by an indoor spotlight. All the other bulbs tested were normal incandescent bulbs. The graph shows a huge jump from zero watts, when the lamp turned off and the photovoltaic cell was being powered by the other lights in the room. The data for the five regular lightbulbs lie along a straight line, suggesting that there is a consistent

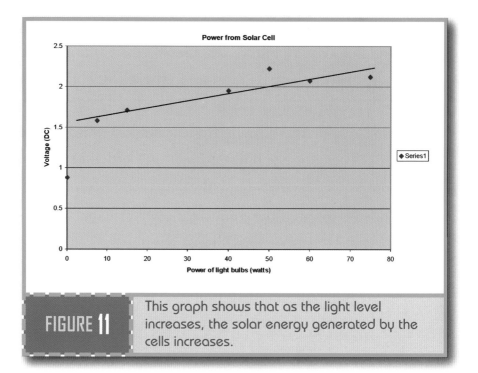

FIGURE 11

This graph shows that as the light level increases, the solar energy generated by the cells increases.

relationship between power in and voltage out. The graph would be more persuasive if there were more data points. That is, it would make a stronger statement if we had used significantly higher wattage lightbulbs: testing a 100-watt and 150-watt bulb, for example. The slope of the straight line is 0.008 volts/watt. For each additional watt of power input, the output voltage increased a tiny fraction of a volt.

Ideas for a Science Fair Project

- If you were going to install a solar cell on the roof of your house to provide electric power, what direction would you face it and at what angle (to the horizon)? Over the course of a sunny day, measure the voltage output from a solar cell at different angles. Graph the voltages vs. the time of day and connect the data for each angle (say for 10, 20, 30, . . . degrees above the horizon). Once you have decided on the optimal angle, use that angle to decide what direction the solar cell should face. Use a compass or GPS to give you the direction.

- Experiment 4.1 showed that changing light levels doesn't have a big impact on the output voltage. You could repeat this experiment using different types of lights and different voltaic cells. Graph your results.

Power an LED With a Photovoltaic Cell

Will the photovoltaic cell power an LED? Keep the lamp off for the first test.

1. Use alligator clip leads to connect an LED to the terminals of the photovoltaic cell. Remember that the LED has to be connected with its positive side (the longer leg) toward the positive (+) terminal of the cell. Does the LED light up?

2. Record this observation in your notebook along with the cell output voltage you measured with the lamp off.

3. Now turn the lamp on. Does the LED light up? Record this observation along with the output voltage. If it didn't light up, can you increase the wattage of the lightbulb to the point where the LED lights up? Record the voltage that turns the LED on.

Things you will need

- **photovoltaic cells**
- **LED**
- **lamp**
- **2 alligator clip leads**
- **experiment notebook**

Connect Two Photovoltaic Cells in a Series Circuit

One engineering problem with solar power is that an individual solar cell generates a very low voltage. In general, this voltage is far below what is needed for most applications. To raise the voltage, several cells are connected together in series.

1. Use an alligator clip lead to connect the positive terminal of one solar cell to the negative terminal of another. Take a second clip lead to connect the positive terminal of the second cell to the red probe of the multimeter. Complete the circuit by clipping the black probe to the negative terminal of the first solar cell.

2. Read and record the output voltage under ambient light (no lamp). Is the voltage higher than you measured using one solar cell?

Things you will need

- 2 photovoltaic cells
- LED
- 3 alligator clip leads
- experiment notebook
- lamp
- multimeter

3. Turn on the lamp to see what voltage this provides. Make sure the light from the lamp is hitting both cells. Record the voltage.

4. If you were unable to power an LED with a single solar cell, try lighting one now with two solar cells. If the LED worked in Experiment 4.2, does it appear brighter this time? (Figure 12.)

FIGURE 12   Two solar cells are powering an LED.

5. Measure the current in this circuit. Use a clip lead to connect the positive multimeter probe to the positive terminal of the first solar cell. Clip the negative probe to the longer leg of an LED. Connect the short LED leg to the negative terminal of the second cell. One clip lead should also be connecting the negative terminal of the first solar cell to the positive terminal of the second cell, thus completing the series circuit. Check to see that the red probe is in the correct receptacle on the meter. Switch the meter to measure current, DCA (direct current amps). Record the current.

6. Now you can calculate the power out and compare it to the power in. To do this, multiply the voltage and current that you have recorded. This will give you power in watts.

   In our experiment, we measured 1.5 volts and 0.02 amps output, giving an electric power of 0.03 watts. To get the power, we multiplied the output voltage by the current (1.5 volts times 0.02 amps). We were using a 75-watt lightbulb to get 0.03 watts output from the cell. That is not an efficient system. However, it isn't as bad as it sounds. Most (90 to 95 percent) of the power produced by the lightbulb is heat and not light. If we assume that the 75-watt lightbulb is working at 3 percent efficiency (based on published data), it is actually generating 2.25 watts of light (75 watts $\times$ 0.03). That makes the photovoltaic cell about 1.3 percent efficient. Further, not all of the light from the bulb is hitting the solar cell. We would have to build a reflective shield around the lamp and solar cell to keep more of the light from escaping.

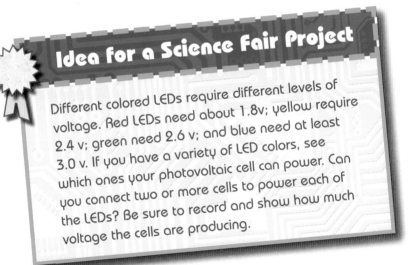

Idea for a Science Fair Project

Different colored LEDs require different levels of voltage. Red LEDs need about 1.8v; yellow require 2.4 v; green need 2.6 v; and blue need at least 3.0 v. If you have a variety of LED colors, see which ones your photovoltaic cell can power. Can you connect two or more cells to power each of the LEDs? Be sure to record and show how much voltage the cells are producing.

Power an Electric Motor With Solar Cells in a Series Circuit

Let's try running an electric motor with the solar cells.

1. Replace the LED (from the previous experiment) with a small electric motor.

2. Can the two photocells power the motor? If not, try more powerful bulbs in the lamp. Try a variety of motors, especially any that require 1v or less. Record your findings.

Things you will need

- 2 photovoltaic cells
- 3 alligator clip leads
- experiment notebook
- DC motor
- lamp

Connect Two Photovoltaic Cells in Parallel

Solar cells also can be connected in parallel. This provides more current, but not more voltage. Since most electrical devices require higher voltage and current than a single solar cell can deliver, many solar cells are wired together. Groups of cells are wired in series to get higher voltages. Several of these groups are wired in parallel to get higher currents. The total output can have much higher voltage and current.

1. Use alligator clip leads to connect the positive terminals or wires of two cells. Use another clip lead to connect the two negative terminals. Now the two cells are in parallel. Can you see the difference from how they were connected (in series) before?

2. Take one more clip lead and connect it to the red probe on the multimeter and to one of the positive terminals on

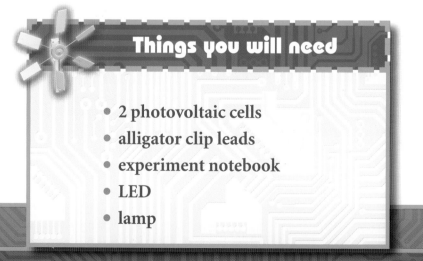

Things you will need

- **2 photovoltaic cells**
- **alligator clip leads**
- **experiment notebook**
- **LED**
- **lamp**

the cells. Connect the negative or black probe to either of the negative terminals.

3. Turn on the light and read the meter. How does this compare to the prior experiment when both were connected in series? Record your observations and voltage measurement.

4. See if the two cells will power an LED. Take the clip leads off both of the multimeter probes and turn the meter off. Where the meter was connected to the cells, insert an LED. The longer leg should be connected to the positive terminals of the two cells. Does it light?

5. If the LED does light, measure the current in the circuit. Connect the red probe of the multimeter to the short leg of the LED with a clip lead. Use one more clip lead to connect the black meter probe to the negative terminals of the two cells. Before turning the meter on to measure the current, check to see if you need to move the plug for the red probe to a different socket.

6. Measure and record the current. Compute the power output by multiplying the voltage by the current. How does the power compare to the power output when the cells were in series?

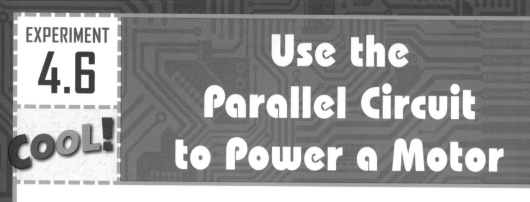

Use the Parallel Circuit to Power a Motor

Knowing how much power the parallel circuit can generate, do you think it can power a motor? Let's give it a try.

1. Connect a small DC electric motor to the parallel circuit of two solar cells (without the multimeter) from Step 1 in Experiment 4.5.

2. Turn on the lamp to see if the cells power the motor.

3. Which circuit (parallel or series from Experiment 4.4) worked better with the motor? Record your observations in your notebook.

Things you will need

- **2 photovoltaic cells**
- **4 alligator clip leads**
- **experiment notebook**
- **LED**
- **lamp**
- **DC electric motor**
- **multimeter**

Make a Solar-Powered Car

Engineering students around the world compete in the World Solar Challenge and the North American Solar Challenge, where they build cars powered by solar arrays. The cars operate on very low power, but with careful engineering, they run well. Most of the cars have three wheels, but some have four. They carry batteries to store excess electric power to use when light levels drop. In these competitions, students try new ideas that could help make solar cars commonplace.

Things you will need

- 1 or 2 photovoltaic cells
- 2 to 4 alligator clip leads
- DC gear-motor assembly
- battery (to test motor)
- small wheels
- dowels (1/8-inch) for axles
- straws for bearings
- hot glue
- cardboard
- craft sticks
- lamps with different wattage bulbs
- test track
- markers
- masking tape
- stopwatch
- camera (optional)
- experiment notebook

FIGURE 13   This car runs on the electricity generated in the two solar cells on top.

Can you use the electricity generated by voltaics to drive a model car? (Figure 13) Could this car operate outdoors on a sunny day? How would you make the car light enough to be powered by solar light?

Think of a design that uses lightweight material and low-friction wheels and bearings. How will you position the voltaic cells to best capture solar energy? How will you get the spinning motion from the motor to the wheels?

Three propulsion systems might work. One is direct drive, where the wheel is mounted directly on motor shaft.

The second is a belt drive, where a rubber band (the belt) carries the motion from the motor shaft to an axle with one or two wheels. The third system uses gears. You can make your own system using gears you purchase, or you can purchase a gear-motor assembly ready to use for solar power.

In making small model cars, we recommend using $^1/_8$-in wood dowels (available from hardware and craft stores and from some science catalogues), plastic wheels that fit on the dowels/axles (check to see that the center wheel opening is $^1/_8$-in), and standard drinking straws for bearings.

1. Glue or tape the straws to the bottom of a rectangle of cardboard (the car frame). Slide the dowels/axles through the straws, and attach the wheels to the dowels.

2. Decide how to get power from the DC motor to the wheels. A geared system works well (see Figure 14). To test the motor and gears, use a battery.

3. Add a platform to hold the photovoltaic cell(s) above the frame. Use craft sticks or other material for the platform and glue them in place.

4. Use alligator clip leads to connect the photovoltaic cells to the motor in a series circuit.

5. Test the car under different lighting conditions.

6. Set up a test track about 3 m (10 ft long) and mark the

start and end lines. Time how long it takes the car to travel the test track. Convert the distance and time into speed (speed is the distance divided by the time it takes to cover that distance), and record this in your experiment notebook.

FIGURE 14

The speed of the motor shaft is reduced in the gear box. The output shaft from the gear box meshes with the drive wheel.

7. Then make changes to your car. You could add more solar cells or switch the circuits to provide more voltage or current. You could also try different ways of getting power to the drive wheels.

For each model you make, record the design and how well (how fast) it does on the test track. If you have a camera available, take a photo of it as well.

Idea for a Science Fair Project

With a solar-powered car, you can conduct a variety of experiments. You could measure its speed (time over a fixed distance) under different lighting conditions. On a clear day you could test it every hour from sunrise to sunset. Or you could use different wattage lightbulbs in handheld lamps directly above the car. You could also try different combinations (series and parallel) of solar cells. Come up with an experiment that will yield numerical values that you can graph for comparing input and output data (such as wattage and speed).

Solar Heaters

A very common use of solar power is for heating water. In some parts of the world, solar heating meets up to 75 percent of a family's hot water needs. In the United States, people with swimming pools use solar heaters (or solar blankets that cut evaporative loss of heat) to heat the pools (see Figure 15).

There is a great variety in the design of solar water heaters. Simplest is to have water flow over a flat panel that is exposed to the sun. The panel is usually painted black to absorb more of the sun's radiation. The water flows over the panel and is heated by contact with the black panel beneath it. Then it is collected at the bottom. More elaborate systems run the water (usually by gravity) through a series of black metal or plastic pipes.

Water heaters use "closed" systems (see Figure 16). The water to be used is

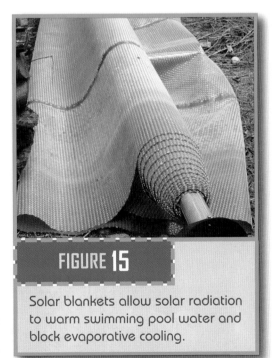

FIGURE 15

Solar blankets allow solar radiation to warm swimming pool water and block evaporative cooling.

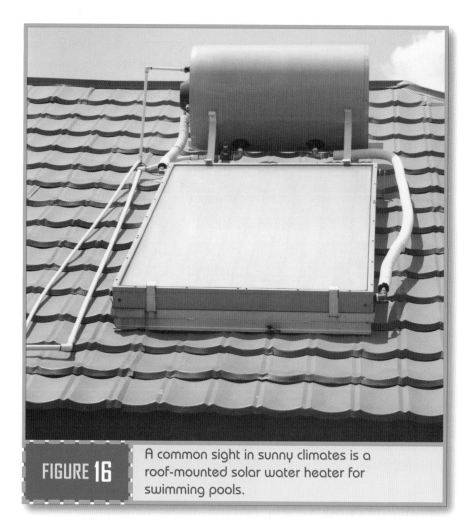

FIGURE 16

A common sight in sunny climates is a roof-mounted solar water heater for swimming pools.

heated by contact with another fluid that flows through the solar collector. Pipes carrying the water and pipes carrying the heating liquid are brought together in a heat exchanger. There, heat moves from the warmer collector fluid to the cooler water used in the house.

Build and Test a Solar Water Heater

You can make and test a solar water heater out of simple materials. An easy way to start is by using a black plastic bag inside a cardboard box. Run small-diameter plastic tubing from a hardware store on top of the black plastic inside the box. Use a funnel to get water into the tube, and collect the water in a plastic bottle at the bottom.

To measure the effectiveness, you will need a thermometer.

Consider a few designs before starting to build. How big you do you want the collector to be? How will you support it so that it faces the sun? Will you run the water through tubes or let it flow directly over the plastic bag? If you live in a dry

Things you will need

- **cooking or laboratory thermometer**
- **2 water containers**
- **black plastic bag**
- **cardboard box**
- **3-meter (10-foot)-length of clear plastic tubing**
- **funnel or cereal box**
- **experiment notebook**

73

or cold region you will want to cover the collector with clear plastic to slow down the evaporative or conductive cooling. If you live in a cold region, also think about insulating the water bottle you use to collect the heated water.

Have you noticed that radiators—in cars, homes, and industrial plants—often have fins? These fins provide a larger surface to promote cooling. You could add heating fins to any tubing you have in your collector. The fins would have to be a dark color to better collect solar radiation, and they would have to be made of a conductive material (metal) so that they transfer the heat to the tubes and water.

1. Start with a container of water and measure its temperature. Let the water sit outside so that its temperature rises or sinks to the ambient conditions. If you take warm water from inside the house and run it through a solar heater that is at a much lower temperature outside, you could find that the water cools in the solar heater rather than warms.

2. While waiting for the thermometer to reach a steady temperature, put the black plastic bag inside the box. Loop the clear tubing in the box as flat and close to the plastic as you can get.

3. After recording the water temperature, pour the water

into the hose. A funnel would help. You can make one out of a cereal box by rolling a flat piece of the cardboard into a cone and cutting a hole at the apex.

4. Collect the water coming out the other end of the tubing and measure its temperature.

5. Record the start and finish temperatures, information on the weather during your experiment, and the length of time that the water was exposed to the sun. If the water didn't warm up significantly, run it through several more times and keep track of how many times you had to recirculate it to get the temperature to rise. If your system uses 3m (10 ft) of plastic tubing for the solar collector, and you had to circulate the water 5 times to get a 2-degree rise in temperature, that would suggest that you would have to increase the length of your tubing to 15m (50 ft) to get a 10-degree rise in temperature. A 10-degree rise would be a great accomplishment!

Make a Non-Circulating Sola Water Heater

1. Use a bag or plastic container to test different ways to improve the collection of solar energy. Measure how quickly water heats up over a 1-hour to 2-hour duration.

2. At the same time on another day, repeat the experiment using a new design to collect more of the sun's energy in order to heat the water faster. Try several different designs. Determine their effectiveness by recording and graphing the time duration and the change in temperature of the water.

Research is being done on how best to collect solar energy over a large area and focus it to heat materials. (See Figure 17.)

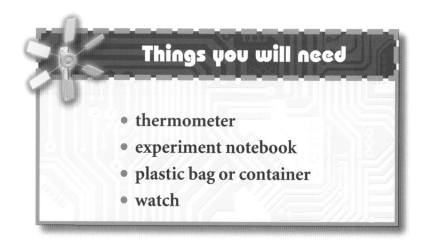

Things you will need

- **thermometer**
- **experiment notebook**
- **plastic bag or container**
- **watch**

FIGURE 17 Mirrors focus solar rays to heat a fluid to create steam. The steam operates a Stirling engine.

Idea for a Science Fair Project

An even easier experiment is to measure how quickly a container of water heats when exposed to the sun. You could use a plastic bag, a recycled soda bottle, or a milk jug to hold the water. Measure the temperature of the water before exposing the container to the sun. Measure the water temperature every ten minutes to see how quickly it warms up. Record the air temperature each time you measure the water temperature. Note the time of day (so you know how high the sun was) and cloud conditions. What could you do to improve the collection of solar energy for this heater?

Wind Power

Solar radiation heats the surface of planet Earth. In turn, the surface heats the air above it. Air that is heated rises in the atmosphere. It also picks up moisture, which rises with the warm air. As Earth spins, air movements generate a complex system of winds. In essence, winds hold solar energy, which we can capture with windmills.

FIGURE 18

Winds have provided power for machinery for centuries. This windmill is in Copenhagen, Denmark.

Windmills have been used to grind grain since the ninth century (see Figure 18). An even earlier use of wind power is the sailboat, which dates back 5,000 years. The idea of using wind power to generate electricity has been around since the nineteenth century, but until the 1980s, it was too costly.

By 2010, wind turbines were being installed in Europe and the United States at a furious pace. Denmark supplies about 20 percent of its electric energy needs from

FIGURE 19

Denmark has wind turbines along the coast and even in the Baltic Sea.

wind (Figure 19). Germany produces the most electricity from wind, and the United States produces the second most (Figure 20). Although U.S. wind generation supplies only a tiny fraction of the total electric power consumed, wind usage is growing 30 percent per year. New materials and technology have lowered the cost of collecting wind energy, while worldwide cost of other energy sources has increased.

FIGURE 20 — These turbines convert wind energy into electricity at a modern wind farm in Montana.

The technological issue with wind power is how to capture it for electricity generation. New methods and designs to capture wind energy are invented every year. Let's start with a basic model.

Make a Sail Car

You can build a car that you can power with sails (see Figure 21). Then experiment with it to find the sail design that makes it go farthest.

1. Use a piece of cardboard for the car body. Hot glue or tape straw pieces to the bottom of the body making sure that they are parallel to each other.

Things you will need

- **an adult**
- **cardboard (for the car body)**
- **glue or tape**
- **straws**
- **wood dowels (1/8-inch diameter for axles, 1/4-inch diameter for mast)**
- **wire cutters**
- **portable electric fan or large sheet of cardboard**
- **wheels (4 plastic wheels, 1-inch diameter; one wooden wheel, 2-inch diameter); or cardboard, drawing compass, and scissors**
- **coping saw**
- **paper or cloth for sails**
- **masking tape**
- **camera (optional)**
- **measuring tape**
- **experiment notebook**

FIGURE 21
Use a fan to propel a sail car. Try different configurations of sails to see which gets the longest run.

2. Use ¹/₈-in dowels as axles. These are available at hardware and craft stores and through science supply catalogs. **Have an adult** use wire cutters to cut the dowels slightly longer than the straws on the bottom of the car.

3. Connect the plastic wheels to the axles. You could also make your own wheels by drawing circles with a compass on cardboard and cutting the wheels out. It is hard to get really round wheels and to find the exact center

unless you use a drawing compass. But both are critical to making a smoothly rolling car. As a third alternative, get old toy cars and either use the wheels or use the car itself.

4. Test your car to ensure that it rolls easily and goes in a straight line. If it doesn't, fix the problem (Are the axles parallel to each other? Is there glue on the axles? Are the wheels rubbing against the body?) before adding a sail.

5. Add a mast. We used $^1/4$-in dowel about 25 cm (10 in) long. **Have an adult** use a coping saw to cut the dowel. Insert it into a wooden wheel with a $^1/4$-in center hole. We glued the wheel to the car body, toward the front of the car. For the sail you can use paper or cloth and figure out how you want to attach it to the mast. The simplest way is to punch two holes in a piece of paper and slide it onto the mast.

6. Set up a test track on a smooth floor. Put a marker (piece of masking tape) down for the start line.

7. If you have a portable electric fan, place it behind the start line and mark its position so that you can always place it in the same position for future experiments. Place the car at the start line and turn on the fan. Measure how far your car goes and record that distance. Ideally you would take a photo of the car and sail so that you know what sail

design gave you the distance you just measured. If a fan isn't available, get a large piece of cardboard and use it as a fan blade. Wave the cardboard like crazy to get the car to move, but don't move the fan beyond the start line. Measure where the car stops, and record the distance traveled before changing the sail design for the next model.

8. Now change the sail design. You might also add a second mast and sail or try the car in reverse. Keep asking yourself questions about how the sail car will work best and then test your ideas by measuring how far the car goes under the influence of the fan.

Idea for a Science Fair Project

Sailing downwind is easy. But can you build a car to sail upwind? Sailboats can sail into the wind— not directly into the wind, but with the air sail at an angle to the wind. Try some sail designs (you might mimic the sails of a modern sailboat) to see how close to the wind you can sail your car. Measure the angle, change the sail design, and try again.

Wind Turbines

Let's take a big jump from the sail technology invented thousands of years ago to modern wind turbines. Wind turbines turn when they are bumped by fast-moving molecules of air (wind). As each molecule hits the blade of a wind turbine, it gives the blade some of its energy. The turbine blade speeds up and the air molecule slows down.

The faster the wind blows, the faster it can spin the turbine blades. What's really impressive is that if the wind speed doubles from 10 to 20 kilometers per hour, the potential power it can deliver to the turbine doesn't just double, it increases 8-fold. Part of the challenge with wind power is finding areas that have consistently strong winds.

The other challenge is extracting as much energy from the wind as possible and converting that into electricity. From the previous experiments, you know how to convert motion into electricity by using a generator. Now let's tackle how to convert wind energy into electricity.

Generate Electricity from the Wind

1. **Ask an adult** to push a cork onto the shaft of a toy motor. If it does not stay on the shaft, put a drop of glue on the shaft and then push the cork on.

2. Draw turbine blades on the bottom of a disposable pie pan. Leave a circle of the pan in the middle so that you can connect the blades to the cork. Cut out the blades using scissors (see Figure 22).

3. Glue the center of the pie pan turbine blade assembly onto the cork. There will be a lot of stress on this connection between cork and pie pan and some glues don't hold well on both surfaces. You may need to try different glues. Start with hot glue and press the surfaces together strongly while the glue sets.

Things you will need

- an adult
- cork
- toy motor
- hot glue
- marker
- disposable pie pan
- scissors
- 2 alligator clip leads
- multimeter
- fan
- experiment notebook

FIGURE 22 — Cut turbine blades from a pie pan and attach them to a motor by gluing them to a cork. Force the cork onto the motor shaft.

4. Connect alligator clip leads to the motor terminals and multimeter probes. Set the dial to measure DC volts in a range that goes up to 20 volts.

5. Turn on the fan and hold the motor in front of it so that the blades can turn freely.

6. Measure and record the voltage output by the turbine.

7. Try other designs and sizes for turbine blades. Try other fans as well and keep good records in your notebook.

Build a Wind Turbine Test Station

The small handheld generator from Experiment 5.2 works well for quick tests of blade designs. But to allow you to do more involved experiments, you will want a self-standing turbine. You could purchase a wind power kit. (See sources in the Appendix.) You could build your own following the procedure below. (See Figure 23.)

1. Start by figuring out how to hold the motor/generator. Take the motor (which will be your generator) to a hardware store and find the size pipe or size of a fitting (an

Things you will need

- **an adult**
- **PVC pipe (8 feet long)**
- **an electric toy motor**
- **1-inch plastic wheel**
- **2-inch wooden wheel**
- **masking tape**
- **electrical tape**
- **duct tape**
- **insulated wire**
- **wire cutters**

- **coping saw**
- **drill and 1/4-inch bit**
- **soldering iron and solder**
- **5 PVC elbows (90-degree bends)**
- **3 PVC T connectors**
- **wood dowels (1/4-inch)**
- **cardboard**
- **balsa wood sheets (1/8-inch thick)**

FIGURE 23 You can try different shapes and sizes of turbine blades to see which generates the most power.

angled piece of PVC) that will hold the motor. If none provide a good, tight fit, pick the size just larger than you need. You can wrap a few layers of masking tape around the outside of the motor to take up space so that the motor fits tightly.

2. Once you know the size of the PVC you will use to hold the motor, collect the other pieces you need.

3. Cut 2 pieces of wire, each about 2 m (7 ft) long.

4. **Ask an adult** to help you solder the wires onto the motor terminals. Up to this point we have used alligator clip leads, but to operate a wind turbine, you need a strong, more reliable connection. If solder isn't available, wrap the uninsulated end of each wire around the motor terminal and tape it in place with electrical tape or masking tape.

5. **Ask the adult** to cut a piece of PVC pipe 9 cm (4 in) long to hold the motor. Before you force the motor into the PVC, run the wires from the motor terminals through the PVC pipe. Then insert the motor with its padding so that the motor shaft sticks out one end and the wires come out the other end. The assembly that holds the motor is called a nacelle (Figure 24).

6. Cut 6 pieces of PVC. Each should be 25 cm (10 in) long.

7. Connect two pieces to the arms of a T connector and two other pieces to a second T connector.

8. Put an elbow (90-degree PVC connector) on each end. The turbine will stand on these elbows.

9. Insert the two remaining 25-cm (10-in)-long pipes into the leg of the Ts.

10. Join these two pieces by connecting the pipe without elbows to the third T. The leg of this T should point upward, and the four elbows should be on the ground.

11. Cut a piece of PVC pipe 76 cm (30 in) long. Insert this into the leg of the third T. This piece will hold the turbine assembly above the ground.

12. Mount the last elbow onto the vertical piece of PVC pipe.

13. Now go back to the nacelle. Run the wires from the motor/generator inside the PVC pipe that houses and supports it so that the ends of the wires come out one of the elbows

FIGURE 24

The nacelle houses the generator and any gearing in a wind turbine.

on the ground. This will keep the wires out of the way of the spinning blades.

14. Push the nacelle into the elbow.

15. Mount the plastic wheel onto the motor shaft. If the hole in the wheel is too large for the motor shaft, you can look in science catalogs for bushings or wrap tape around the motor shaft and force the wheel over the tape.

16. **Have an adult** drill four $1/4$-in holes equally spaced around the edge of the wooden wheel.

17. Glue the larger wooden wheel to the plastic wheel.

18. Cut four 10-in-long pieces of the ¼-in dowel. Insert them into the holes in the edge of the wheel.

19. Cut four turbine blades out of single-ply cardboard (from cereal boxes). For your first design, make the blades about 20 cm (8 in) long and 5 to 7 cm (2 to 3 in) wide. Using cardboard allows you to try different shapes and sizes easily. When you find a design that works well, you can use them as patterns for cutting out more durable blades from $1/8$-in balsa wood.

20. Use duct tape to mount the blades onto the dowels. Tape will allow you to change the angle that blades make to the wind. You are ready to test your turbine.

Test Your Wind Turbine

1. Connect the wires coming from the wind turbine to an LED. Remember to connect the long leg of the LED to the positive side of the turbine. If the LED doesn't light even when the turbine is turning, try switching the connections on the LED.

2. Position the fan in front of the turbine and turn it on. Adjust the angle of the turbine blades to get the most rapid spinning. If the turbine isn't spinning, first check to see that it is free to spin—that nothing is holding it in place. If it spins when you turn it, you might need a more powerful fan. If the LED is lighting up, you are generating electricity. Congratulations!

Things you will need

- **wind turbine and stand (purchased or built in Experiment 5.3)**
- **2 alligator clip leads**
- **LED**
- **fan**
- **experiment notebook**

Measure the Voltage Output

Let's find out how much electricity you are making.

1. Connect a voltmeter or multimeter to the wires coming from the turbine generated electricity.

2. Switch the meter to measure volts (DC or DCV) in the range of 20 volts.

3. Record the output voltage in your experiment notebook.

4. Measure the distance from the fan to the turbine. Record that information (don't forget to include the units of measurement: centimeters, meters, inches, or feet). Also record the fan settings you are using: high, low, medium, or other settings.

5. How fast is your turbine turning? Notice the speed. Mark one of the blades with a marker. With the help of a friend, count the number of times the marked blade rotates in 30 seconds. Double this number to get revolutions per minute. Record this so that you can compare it to its speed in the next experiment.

See the Effect of Adding a Load to the Circuit

What happens if you put a load on the turbine? That is, what does the turbine do if you connect the output wires to an LED or motor? Remember how fast it was turning in the last experiment. There, it was generating electricity without having to power a motor or LED. Remember that when you measured the voltage in a non-running battery, it was higher than the voltage in the same battery that was powering a motor. Adding a load will make the generator work harder, and you will see a drop in voltage.

1. Connect an LED to the output wires, making sure that you have it connected so it will light when the turbine spins. Turn the fan on and notice that the LED is on.

Things you will need

- **wind turbine and stand (from Experiment 5.5)**
- **fan**
- **LED**
- **DC motor**
- **2 alligator clip leads**
- **experiment notebook**

If so, again count the number of revolutions the turbine blades make in 30 seconds and double it to get revolutions per minute. Is this number different from the number you recorded in the previous experiment?

2. See if your turbine will power a toy motor. Replace the LED with a motor. Does the motor spin? If so, count the number of revolutions the turbine blades rotate in a minute.

3. Record both measurements in your experiment note-book. Why did the turbine slow when you connected it to the LED or motor?

As electric generators take on increasing loads, they work harder. Just like a battery with no load, it is easy for a generator to show a high voltage when it is doing no work. But when either a battery or generator is connected to a load, the voltage drops.

How Much Power Is Your Turbine Generating?

Measure the current that your wind turbine is generating. As we found in Experiment 3.5, power is the product of the voltage and current (Power = Voltage × Current). Knowing both the voltage and current output will let you calculate how much power the wind generator is producing.

1. Wire an LED in series with the turbine and the meter. Using alligator clip leads, connect one of the meter probes to one wire from the generator. Connect the other meter probe to one of the legs of an LED. A third wire connects the other LED leg to the other generator wire. Now, as long as the LED is inserted in the correct direction, current will be able to flow from the generator through

Things you will need

- **wind turbine and stand**
- **fan**
- **multimeter**
- **LED**
- **DC motor**
- **3 alligator clip leads**
- **experiment notebook**

the meter and LED and back to the generator—making a complete circuit.

2. Record the current along with the voltage and other information you collected in the previous experiment.

3. Calculate the power from the values of voltage (Experiment 5.5) and current (this experiment). If your turbine is producing 0.5 volt and 0.02 amp, its power output is 0.01 watts.

4. Check out the wattage of the lightbulbs in your house. You can find the wattage listed on the box a bulb comes in and on the top of the bulb itself. (Be careful not to grab a bulb that is turned on as it will be hot. Incandescent bulbs generate more heat than light.) Your model generator couldn't power even one of the standard household lights. To get more power, you will have to either build a much bigger generator or speed up the rotation of the generator shaft.

Use a Geared Turbine

The motors you are using to generate electricity can spin very rapidly, up to a few thousand revolutions per minute. The faster they spin, the more power they will generate. Without gears, the generator is spinning at a tiny fraction of its top speed. By adding gears between the turbine blades and the generator, you can improve the energy output.

Some wind turbine kits come with a gear box (Figure 25). You can make a gear box yourself—although it isn't easy to get it to work well. It is difficult to attach the gears to a rigid surface at exactly the correct spacing so that they mesh with adjacent gears. One way to solve this problem is to get mounting brackets for gears and motors. These are sheets of plastic with precut holes that you can use to support axles, motor shafts, and gears. If you have a drill press

Things you will need

- **geared turbine or geared motor and stand**
- **LED**
- **2 alligator clip leads**
- **fan**
- **multimeter**

available (and **an adult** to help you), you can make your own mounting brackets out of light metal or plastic.

The model shown in Figure 25 has one pair of gears with the large gear attached to the axle of the turbine. It drives a small gear that is on the shaft of the generator. Large gears driving small gears increase the rate of turning. In this case, the gear ratio is about 3.5 to 1. Every time the large gear (and the turbine blades) makes one revolution, the smaller gear (and generator shaft) makes nearly 3.5 revolutions.

FIGURE 25 This gear box increases the speed of rotation for the generator.

This gearing system will speed up the rotation of the generator 3.5 times.

1. Replace the motor used in your test station with a geared motor. Make sure that the gearing increases the rotation rate of the motor's output. With you fingers, turn the motor shaft one revolution and count how many times the gear on the output shaft turns. It should turn several times.

2. Set up the turbine, multimeter, LED, and fan as you did in Experiment 5.7. Be sure to set the fan at the distance you used in the previous experiment so that you can compare the effect of the gearing system on the power output under the same "wind" conditions.

3. Measure the output voltage and the current. Calculate the power output. How does this compare with the power produced before?

   Companies are now selling home wind power turbines and generators so that people can make their own electricity and not have to buy it from a supplier. Do an online search for home wind generators and see how much interest there is in this. Other companies are building wind farms and selling the electricity to companies that supply homes and industry. This is a fast-growing field—one that could benefit from your creative new design for wind collectors.

Ideas for a Science Fair Project

■ Once you have a turbine and wind source set up, you can evaluate different propeller designs. Make your own designs out of stiff disposable dinner plates or disposable aluminum pie pans. Figure out a way to measure the area of each propeller design you make. One way would be to weigh each propeller on a scale at school and, assuming each propeller is made of the same material, the weights would give you a relative measure of the surface area of the propellers. Compare each to the weight of a complete plate or pan before cutting to see the percentage of the total area each propeller has. Or, compare propellers with the same area but different numbers of blades. Is a propeller with two wide blades more effective than one with four narrower ones? What else could you test?

■ The wind turbines we have used all rotate like a typical house fan, with the blades spinning around a horizontal axis. But there are other designs for you to try (see Figure 26). Wind turbines that rotate around a vertical axis are very efficient. You could compare the two different turbine designs (vertical versus horizontal axis) for a science fair project.

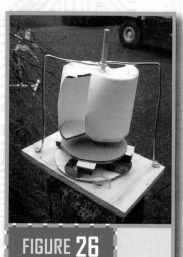

FIGURE 26

A different design for wind turbines uses this Savonius rotor design.

Hydropower

ong before people knew about the power of electricity, they were using water power, or hydropower. Earliest references to waterwheels date from about 6,000 years ago in Greece. Other cultures developed their own ways to use the power in water moving down rivers or streams.

The first application of hydropower was probably raising water from a river or stream so that it could flow into a field to irrigate it. Later, people created new designs to take advantage of the power of a river to provide power for a variety of agricultural and industrial purposes. Water power was used to grind grain, treat cloth, and tan hides. Saw-mills and metalworking mills were also powered by water. Several water-powered mills continue to operate in the United States, including Birkenhead Mills at the Hagley Museum and Library on the Brandywine River in Wilmington, Delaware (Figure 27).

Today, watermills look quaint, but we use electricity generated from hydropower extensively. Nearly 20 percent of the world's electricity is generated by hydropower.

In the United States, hydropower is associated with

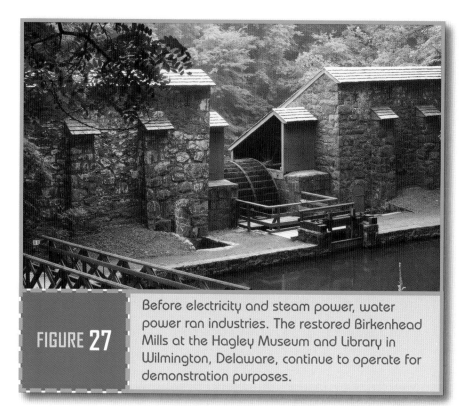

FIGURE 27

Before electricity and steam power, water power ran industries. The restored Birkenhead Mills at the Hagley Museum and Library in Wilmington, Delaware, continue to operate for demonstration purposes.

massive dams holding back the water collected in reservoirs (Figure 28). However, micro-hydro plants are becoming increasingly popular. Both large and small plants operate under the same principles. Water, carried by clouds and deposited on high-elevation lands, collects in lakes and rivers. Its natural path downstream and back to the ocean is interrupted by a dam or other device to collect and hold the water. A pipe (penstock) brings gravity-fed water to lower elevations, where it turns a turbine that runs a generator.

The power generated by a dam depends on the amount of water available and the height of the dam. The vertical distance the water falls is called the head. The greater the head, the more potential energy there is available. Regions in the United States with mountains and consistent rainfall, like the Pacific Northwest, have many hydroelectric power plants.

With hydropower, there is no cost for fuel, and the fuel is constantly renewable. The reservoirs created to hold water also make great places for people to water-ski, fish, and enjoy other aquatic activities. That's great, but there are disadvantages as well.

It's difficult to increase the supply of energy produced by existing hydroelectric projects. Building dams is very expensive (it may take as long as a decade of generating electricity to pay for building the dam) and has high environmental impacts. Blocking the flow of water in a river robs the lower sections of the river of silt and sediment carried by the river, which are deposited in the still water of the reservoir. Robbed of sediment, downstream riverbanks erode. The dam also blocks fish and other aquatic life from moving upstream and downstream. Fish ladders can help alleviate the problem, but only for species that can find and navigate the ladders. Dams also interrupt the seasonal cycles of the river or stream. Reservoirs hold water for use throughout the year and release

FIGURE 28

The second highest dam in the United States, Hoover Dam supplies water to drive 17 generators, which produce over 2,000 megawatts of electrical power. Photo provided by US Bureau of Reclamation.

water downstream as electricity is generated, at a somewhat constant rate. But many streams and rivers naturally have huge fluctuations in water volume and energy. Stopping these fluctuations changes the environment below the dam. Above the dam, where a reservoir has replaced a natural river or stream, the environment is radically changed. Large land areas become submerged by the reservoir. Water temperature and oxygen levels also are changed, which directly affects the ecology in the water and on the land around it. Dams are very disruptive to native plant and animal species.

With all these benefits and disadvantages, large dams are very controversial. However, small-scale hydroelectric plants can provide electricity in remote locations with minimal impact on the environment.

Let's try capturing some hydropower with a waterwheel. There are several waterwheel designs. The oldest and least efficient is an undershot wheel. Think of a waterwheel mounted vertically in a river. As the river runs downstream, it pushes against the bottom of the wheel. The wheel turns only as fast as the river runs. Undershot wheels capture only about 20 percent of the available energy.

For an overshot wheel, the water comes in from above the wheel in a sluice or trough. The water spills out of the sluice and hits the top of the wheel as it falls. Both the downstream momentum of the water and the energy transmitted as it falls help drive the wheel. This wheel is about 70 percent efficient.

In a breastshot wheel, water is carried in by a sluice and hits the wheel about halfway from the top. Instead of having paddles on the edge of the wheel to capture the energy of the passing water, a breastshot wheel has bucketlike containers. It delivers less energy (50 percent) than the overshot wheel. It was used on large-volume rivers that have steady flow.

Make an Overshot Waterwheel

Waterwheels are wheels with structures on them to capture moving water. These structures can be buckets, paddles, or blades.

1. An easy way to make a waterwheel is to use plastic spoons for buckets. What can you use as a wheel to hold the spoons? The simplest way would be to use a piece of rigid

Things you will need

- an adult
- plastic spoons
- rigid foam or a hollow sports ball
- pencil, piece of coat hanger, or a wood dowel
- milk shake straws
- 2 or 3 tennis balls or racquet balls
- experiment notebook
- hacksaw (to cut the spoon handles)
- sheet of paper
- scissors
- ruler
- vise
- hole saw (3-inch diameter)
- coping saw
- tape
- hot glue or adhesive
- file or sandpaper
- 1-inch-thick pine board
- watch
- hose or sink
- a partner
- camera (optional)

foam (Figure 29). Carefully push a pencil, piece of coat hanger, or dowel through the center for an axle.

FIGURE 29

This simple wheel spins when placed under a faucet.

2. **Ask an adult** to cut the plastic spoon handles to the desired length with a hack saw. Stick the spoon bowls into the edges of the foam block at evenly spaced intervals.

3. Hold this under a faucet so the stream of water falls on the bowls to have it spin on its axle. To allow the axle to turn easier, slide a large diameter straw over each end of the axle and hold the straw. A stronger model would use a tennis ball or racquetball.

4. Mark a great circle or equator around a tennis ball or racquetball and decide how many buckets you want to mount on the ball.

5. Cut a strip of paper 1 cm (1/2 in) wide and 25 cm (10 in) long. Wrap this around the equator of the ball. Cut the paper where it overlaps the end so that the paper length matches the length of the equator. Use a ruler to measure

FIGURE 30

FIGURE 30

The plastic spoons of this wheel, when held under a faucet or hose, can capture the energy of falling water and spin the wheel.

the length of the paper strip and divide by the number of buckets. Using this measurement, mark the paper to give you the spacing for the buckets. Then tape the strip onto the ball along the equator.

6. **With adult help**, cut the ball at the marks on the paper. You want the spoons to fit tightly in the ball so that they don't come out when water hits them.

7. **Ask an adult** to cut the plastic spoon handles to the desired length with a hack saw. Put several in a vise so that they are all cut at once. Insert the bowls (handle first) into the ball.

8. If the line you drew on the ball is the equator, find the north and south poles. Poke a hole through both poles to run an axle through it (use a piece of a coat hanger or a wood dowel).

If you have access to woodworking tools, here is another approach to making a waterwheel.

1. **With adult help** cut a circle out of 1-in-thick pine board with a 3-in hole saw (see Figure 30).

2. **Ask an adult** to cut the plastic spoon handles to the desired length with a hack saw. Put several in a vise so that they are all cut at once. Insert the bowls (handle first) into the ball.

3. Draw four diameters, equally spaced, across one side of the wood circle. These will show you where to make cuts for 8 spoons. With the wooden wheel in a vise, use a coping saw to cut slots at each mark. Cut these straight across the edge of the wheel and cut them slightly narrower than the piece of the handle that is still attached to the bowl of the spoons. Use a file or sandpaper to widen the slots so that the spoon handles will fit in.

4. Coat the end of each spoon with a good adhesive (hot glue will hold, but other epoxy adhesives will last longer) and jam them into each of the 8 slots. Be sure the spoons face the same direction. After the glue has dried, slide a pencil through the center hole so that the wheel can spin freely. The waterwheel is ready to test.

5. To test your waterwheel, hold it by the axle. Slide straw

pieces over the axle and hold those if that helps it spin more freely.

6. Place the edge of one of the spoon bowls under a running faucet in a large sink that will catch most of the splashed water. Or, take it outside and use a garden hose.

7. Notice how fast the waterwheel turns. Mark one spoon by wrapping a piece of tape around it. With help from a friend, count how many times the wheel spins in 15 seconds by watching the taped spoon pass a point.

8. Try moving either the water source or the wheel to different positions to find the best relative position (fastest spinning). Try running the waterwheel backward—having the water hit the spoons on the back side rather than in the bowl. Record your observations, along with a photo of your testing procedure, in your experiment notebook.

Idea for a Science Fair Project

Would your waterwheel work better if the buckets were larger? Could you glue, tape, or clip some additional material to the spoons to make them bigger? Would it work as well with fewer or more spoons? Ask some great questions about how to make it work better and then run an experiment. Be sure to record your results.

Make a Hydroelectric Generator

You can make your own hydroelectric generator and test it at home. If you live near a stream, you might be able to operate it there as well. To make a hydrogenerator, we will use the same approach we used in Experiment 5.2 to generate electricity from the wind. Use the waterwheel you made in Experiment 6.1 to make a hydroelectric generator

1. Replace the axle of your waterwheel with a 20-cm (8-in)-long wood dowel.

2. **With adult help**, drill a tiny hole in one end of the axle.

3. Put a dab of glue on the shaft of the motor and force the shaft into the hole you drilled in the axle.

Things you will need

- **an adult**
- **waterwheel from Experiment 6.1**
- **¼-inch wood dowel, 20 cm (8 in) long**
- **milk shake straw**
- **experiment notebook**
- **multimeter**
- **drill**
- **glue**
- **toy motor**
- **2 alligator clip leads**

4. Connect the motor terminals to the probes of the multimeter. Turn the meter to read volts, DC.

5. Slide the straw onto the other end of the dowel so that you can hold the waterwheel at that end. One hand will hold the motor, and the other hand will hold the straw. The straw will let you support the axle as it spins.

6. Keeping the meter away from water, hold the waterwheel under a faucet.

7. Read the meter to see if you are generating electricity. Record your results.

8. Move the wheel higher and lower in the stream of falling water to find the place where the most electricity is generated.

Make a Geared Waterwheel

Water falling from a faucet might not be able to spin the generator fast enough to generate electricity, so add at least one pair of gears. You need to have a large gear mounted on the axle that supports the waterwheel. It will drive a smaller gear mounted on the motor/generator shaft. If you have gears from Experiment 5.8 you can use them here. If you want to purchase gears or a gear assembly already made, look for gears that will spin the motor/generator shaft 10 times for each time the water-wheel spins. This is called a 10:1 gear ratio.

1. Pull the motor shaft out of the end of the axle.

2. Insert the shaft for the large gear into the axle.

3. Push a small gear onto the motor shaft so that it can be turned by the larger gear.

4. Test this gear waterwheel by following the procedures in Experiment 6.2. Record your results. Did the gears increase the output voltage?

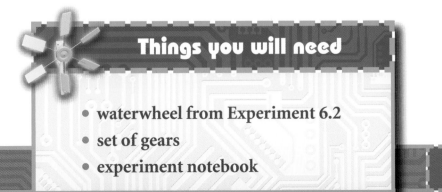

Things you will need

- **waterwheel from Experiment 6.2**
- **set of gears**
- **experiment notebook**

Idea for a Science Fair Project

Make your own gear box that allows you to try different gear ratios with your waterwheel. Kelvin Educational (see Appendix) and other science supply companies sell the gears, metal shafts, and plastic grids that allow you to assemble your own gear box. You could try multiple gears to speed up the rotation of the motor. Calculate the gear ratio by counting the number of teeth on each pair of gears (Figure 31). If one gear has 10 teeth and it meshes with a gear having 50 teeth, this gear set has a ratio of 5:1. You can verify the ratio by marking each gear and counting how many times the smaller gear spins for each spin of the larger gear. Record the gear ratios and the voltage output by your waterwheel. If you make and test several different gear boxes, you could graph the results to show how the voltage output varies with different gear ratios.

FIGURE 31 To find out what the gear ratio is, you can either count the number of times the small gear turns for each revolution of the large gear, or count the teeth on each gear and calculate the ratio.

Increase the Head and Measure the Output Voltage

The power generated by a hydroelectric generator depends directly on the distance water falls (or the height of the water above the turbine) before it impacts the waterwheel. In this experiment, you get to try increasing the distance that water falls. Get some help from someone to hold the multimeter, keeping it dry and taking readings.

1. Connect the hose to an outside faucet. Lay the end of the hose on the bottom rung of a step ladder, or ask a friend to hold the hose.

2. Have another friend hold the multimeter and record voltages.

Things you will need

- garden hose
- waterwheel from either Experiment 6.2 or 6.3, connected to a multimeter
- step ladder
- yardstick or meterstick
- 2 alligator clip leads
- experiment notebook
- 1 or 2 partners

3. Turn on the water and let it hit the spoons in the waterwheel. Move the waterwheel around to find the spot where you get the largest voltage. Record this voltage and the distance of the hose above the waterwheel. This distance is called the head.

4. Move the hose to the next higher rung of the ladder and repeat the measurement.

5. Make as many measurements of voltage and head as you can.

6. Graph this data with the head on the horizontal axis and the output voltage on the vertical axis. Does the data fall along a straight line?

The power available to drive the generator increases linearly with increasing head. Thus, on a graph of power vs. head, we would expect the data to be (more or less) a straight line or to be linear. One unit increase in height causes one unit increase in power. However, there are several other factors that could influence the data you collected and the graph you drew.

In this experiment you measured voltage output, not power output and there could be some difference between the two. As you raised the water source, the falling water probably spread out, so some of it didn't hit the blades on the waterwheel. It may have even hit some blades on the back side of the waterwheel, thus slowing it down. If your data did not give a nice straight line, see if you can figure out why.

Idea for a Science Fair Project

Try different paddle configurations to see which generates the most power (Figure 32). Does increasing the number of blades or the size of the blades improve the power output? Keep good records of each experiment and represent your data in a graph, showing the output power vs. the number or size of the blades.

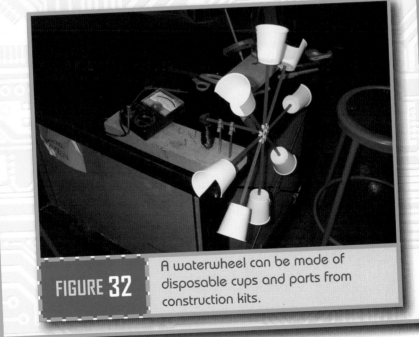

FIGURE 32 A waterwheel can be made of disposable cups and parts from construction kits.

Appendix

Sources for Wind Power Kits

Kelvin Educational
<http://www.kelvin.com>

Kid Wind
<http://www.kidwind.org>

Glossary

alternating current (AC)—The flow of electrons that reverses direction at regular intervals. Household electricity has alternating current; it changes direction with a frequency of 60 cycles per second in the United States.

Ampere (or amps)—A unit of electric current flow. The name honors an early electrical researcher, André-Marie Ampère, who discovered electromagnetism. One amp is approximately 6.24×1018 electrons moving past a point in a second.

circuit—A closed loop through which electrons can flow from a source and back to the source.

coalification—The process of creating coal. It involves biological, physical, and chemical processes over thousands of years.

direct current (DC)—The flow electrons in one direction. Electrons leave the source, move through a circuit, and return to the source, always moving in the same direction. Batteries supply DC current.

enriched uranium—A form of uranium that has a higher percentage of the uranium isotope 235 than is found naturally. It is the fuel used in nuclear power plants. The uranium is enriched to increase the radiation it delivers in the reactor.

heat exchanger—A device that allows the transfer heat from one material to another. A radiator is a heat exchanger.

light-emitting diode (LED)—An electronic component (diode) that passes electricity in only one direction. When current is flowing through an LED, it converts some of the electrical energy directly into light.

nacelle—Part of a wind turbine. It houses the generator, gears, and circuitry.

parallel circuit—An electrical circuit in which two or more components have the same voltage. Connecting two batteries together so that the positive terminal of one is connected the positive terminal of the other battery and that the negative terminals are connected together is an example of a parallel circuit wiring.

photons—Particles that carry the energy of electromagnetic radiation, including light. One photon is the basic unit of light.

photovoltaics—The technology of developing solar cells to capture and convert sunlight into electricity.

radiation—Energy in the form of high-speed particles and waves.

renewable energy—Energy derived from sources that are replenished naturally on short time scales. Although coal and oil are naturally occurring energy sources, they require long time periods to be replenished.

series circuit—An electric circuit or connection in which the terminal of one device (motor, battery, light, etc.) is connected to a terminal of the adjacent device so that the entire circuit is connected from one to the other, end to end.

volt—A measure of the electrical force available. It is named for Italian scientist Alessandro Volta, who invented the battery.

watt—A unit of power or energy flow. The unit honors the inventor of the (improved) steam engine, James Watt. A circuit that delivers one amp of current at one volt has a power of one watt. In most applications, power is measured in units of 1,000 watts (kilowatts).

Further Reading

Fridell, Ron. *Earth-Friendly Energy*. Minneapolis: Lerner Publications, 2009.

Thomas, Isabel. *The Pros and Cons of Solar Power*. New York: Rosen Central, 2008.

VanCleave, Janice. *Janice VanCleave's Energy for Every Kid*. Hoboken, N.J.: J. Wiley and Sons, 2006.

Walter, Niki. *Hydrogen: Running on Water*. New York: Crabtree Publishers, 2006.

Internet Addresses

Super Science Fair Projects
<http://www.super-science-fair-projects.com/
energy-science-fair-projects.html>

U.S. Department of Energy. "EERE: Kids Home Page."
<http://www.eere.energy.gov/kids/>

U.S. Energy Information Administration. "EIA Energy Kids."
<http://tonto.eia.doe.gov/kids/>

Index